STUDENT BOOK

DiSCOVeR how to grow SPiRiTUAllY and why it matters

Michelle Gritter

FAITH ALIVE®
Christian Resources

Grand Rapids, Michigan

CRC Publications thanks Michelle Gritter for writing this course.
Michelle is an ordained minister in the Christian Reformed
Church serving as campus pastor at Abbotsford Christian
Secondary School in British Columbia.

Faith Alive Christian Resources published by CRC Publications.
Discover How to Grow Spiritually and Why It Matters. Church
school material for early teens, © 2000, CRC Publications, 2850
Kalamazoo Ave. SE, Grand Rapids, MI 49560. All rights
reserved. Printed in the United States of America on recycled
paper.

We welcome your comments. Call us at 1-800-333-8300 or
e-mail us at editors@faithaliveresources.

ISBN 1-56212-523-0

10 9 8 7 6 5 4 3 2

Where Am I?

The Story of the Lost Son ◄ • • • • • • • • • • • • • • •

Luke 15:11-32, New International Reader's Version

[11]There was a man who had two sons. [12]The younger son spoke to his father. He said, "Father, give me my share of the family property." So the father divided his property between his two sons.

[13]Not long after that, the younger son packed up all he had. Then he left for a country far away. There he wasted his money on wild living. [14]He spent everything he had.

Then the whole country ran low on food. So the son didn't have what he needed. [15]He went to work for someone who lived in that country, who sent him to the fields to feed the pigs. [16]The son wanted to fill his stomach with the food the pigs were eating, but no one gave him anything.

[17]Then he began to think clearly again. He said, "How many of my father's hired workers have more than enough food! But here I am dying from hunger! [18]I will get up and go back to my father. I will say to him, 'Father, I have sinned against heaven. And I have sinned against you. [19]I am no longer fit to be called your son. Make me like one of your hired workers.'" [20]So he got up and went to his father.

While the son was still a long way off, his father saw him. He was filled with tender love for his son. He ran to him. He threw his arms around him and kissed him. [21]The son said to him, "Father, I have sinned against heaven and against you. I am no longer fit to be called your son."

[22]But the father said to his servants, "Quick! Bring the best robe and put it on him. Put a ring on his finger and sandals on his feet. [23]Bring the fattest calf and kill it.

Let's have a big dinner and celebrate. [24]This son of mine was dead. And now he is alive again. He was lost. And now he is found."

So they began to celebrate.

[25]The older son was in the field. When he came near the house, he heard music and dancing. [26]So he called one of the servants. He asked him what was going on.

[27]"Your brother has come home," the servant replied. "Your father has killed the fattest calf. He has done this because your brother is back safe and sound."

[28]The older brother became angry. He refused to go in. So his father went out and begged him.

[29]But he answered his father, "Look! All these years I've worked like a slave for you. I have always obeyed your orders. You never gave me even a young goat so I could celebrate with my friends. [30]But this son of yours wasted your money with some prostitutes. Now he comes home. And for him you kill the fattest calf!"

[31]"My son," the father said, "you are always with me. Everything I have is yours. [32]But we had to celebrate and be glad. This brother of yours was dead. And now he is alive again. He was lost. And now he is found."

What's Happening in the Story?

Go back and read the story of the lost son from page 2. As you read, fill in the chart on this page. For each character that's listed on the chart, jot down the location and the feelings of the character. The first line has been completed for you.

Character	Location	Feelings
Father	At home with both sons	Happy to be with his sons
Younger son		
Older brother		

On the Journey

Today you were asked to "step into" the story of the lost son and find your place with one of the characters in one of the scenes of the story. You were asked to do this to help you think about where you are on your own spiritual journey. Please take time now to jot down WHY you most identify with the character and location you chose.

I chose to identify with

_____

[name of character]

as he was

_____

[location and what character was doing]

because ...

"For most of my life I have struggled to find God, to know God, to love God. I have tried hard to follow the guidelines of the spiritual life—pray always, work for others, read the Scriptures. . . . I have failed many times but always tried again, even when I was close to despair.

Now I wonder whether I have sufficiently realized that during all this time God has been trying to find me, to know me, and to love me. The question is not, 'How am I to find God?' but, 'How am I to let myself be found by him?' The question is not, 'How am I to know God?' but, 'How am I to let myself be known by God?' And finally the question is not, 'How am I to love God?' but, 'How am I to let myself be loved by God?' God is looking into the distance for me, trying to find me, and longing to bring me home."

—Henri J. M. Nouwen, The Return of the Prodigal Son:
A Story of Homecoming, Doubleday, 1992, page 106

Connected To Jesus

Peter's Up-and-Down Connection to Jesus

How to Use the Connect-o-Graph:

☞ Working with one or two partners, use a Bible to read the stories listed along the bottom of the Connect-o-Graph. Each of the stories is about the relationship between Peter and Jesus. Start with the story on the left and move toward the right.

☞ After you read each story, decide together how strong the relationship between Jesus and Peter was at that time. Was it very weak, fairly weak, just OK, fairly strong, or very strong? Indicate your choice with a dot on the Connect-o-Graph. Each partner fills out his or her own graph. If you disagree with each other, just do what you think is best.

☞ In the space provided below each of the passages listed, write a sentence or two explaining why you put your dot where you did. Later on you will be asked to explain some of your choices, so be sure to do this activity thoughtfully.

☞ Move on to the next passage and repeat the process until you reach the end of the stories. Do not do "My Story" at this time.

☞ Take a ruler or other straight edge and connect the dots on your Connect-o-Graph. If you wish, tear out pages 8 and 9 and tape them together.

STRENGTH OF
THE CONNECTION

Connect

VERY STRONG

FAIRLY STRONG

JUST OKAY

FAIRLY WEAK

VERY WEAK

1. Matthew
4:18-20
(The Calling)

2. Matthew
14:22-32
(Walking on Water)

3. Matthew
16:13-19
(The Confession)

4. Matthew
16:21-25
(The Rebuke)

o-Graph

5. Matthew 17:1-9 *(The Transfiguration)*	6. John 13:31-38 *(The Boast)*	7. John 18:15-18, 25-27 *(The Denial)*	8. John 21:15-19 *(The Restoration)*	My Story

Group 1: *Can anything ever separate us from Christ's love?*

Group 2: *Does it mean he no longer loves us if we have trouble or calamity,*

Group 1: *or are persecuted, or are hungry or cold or in danger or threatened with death?*

Group 2: *No, despite all these things, overwhelming victory is ours through Christ, who loved us.*

Group 1: *I am convinced that NOTHING can EVER separate us from Christ's love.*

Group 2: *Death can't, and life can't.*

Group 1: *The angels can't, and the demons can't.*

Group 2: *Our fears for today, our worries about tomorrow, and even the powers of hell can't keep God's love away.*

Group 1: *Whether we are high above the sky*

Group 2: *or in the deepest ocean,*

Group 1: *NOTHING in all creation*

Group 2: *NOTHING in all creation will EVER be able to separate us*

All: *from the love of God that is revealed in Christ Jesus our Lord.*

—Romans 8:35, 37-39 (based on the New Living Translation)

Getting into the Word

Seven Stumpers

These are well-known sayings disguised in flowery language. How many can you figure out?

1. Exaggerated high opinions of oneself precede a tumble.

_____

_____

2. It is difficult to ascertain the contents of a volume by merely scanning its outer appearance.

_____

_____

3. A chronic disposition to inquiry once deprived a domestic feline—a carnivorous quadruped—of its vital quality.

_____

_____

4. Immediately upon the absence of the domestic feline, carnivorous quadrupeds—common house rodents—proceed to engage in sportive capers.

_____

_____

5. Each nimbo-stratus is graced with an inner surface of argentum.

6. Endeavor not to number your flock of the family *Phasianidae* until the ovoid-shaped objects of their labor have opened to reveal their contents.

_____

_____

7. When an amicable acquaintance offers assistance while you are in dire straits, he is truly not a foe.

_____

_____

My Top Three Benefits of Daily Bible Reading

1. _____
   _____
   _____
   _____

2. _____
   _____
   _____
   _____

3. _____
   _____
   _____
   _____

Three Plans for Daily Bible Reading

On the pages that follow are three plans that will help you read your Bible each day—and grow closer to God.

• • • • • • • • • • • • ➤

Plan A:
Cry of My Heart— Meditating on the Psalms

What This Is About

In this three-week program, you will be reading one psalm a day. This program will help you express what's in your heart when you pray to God, no matter what your mood might be. It will help you listen to God speak to you as you read and think about verses from the Bible.

Set a goal of daily Bible study for the next three weeks. If for some reason you miss a day or two, don't quit the program! Just pick up where you left off and keep going until the three weeks are up. Remember that the goal isn't to rack up Bible study time to impress God, your accountability partner, or anyone else! The goal is to get to know God better by listening to God speak to you.

What You Will Need

- a quiet, comfortable, private place

- a Bible (you may want to use an easy-to-understand version like the New Living Translation)

- a pen and journal

- about fifteen to twenty minutes of your day

- a willingness to listen to God

The Plan

1. Find a quiet, comfortable, private place where you can read, pray, and write in your journal.

2. Spend a minute or two quieting down. Close your eyes and take some slow, deep breaths. Sometimes listening to a soothing song can help you relax.

3. Pray. Ask God to meet you today. Ask God to help you say what's on your heart. Ask God to help you listen as God speaks to you through the Word and Spirit.

4. Choose a psalm to read. You may choose a psalm from the chart on the back of this page or just start with Psalm 1 and work your way forward through the whole book of Psalms. If you find that you don't understand what a psalm is saying, don't worry! Just move on to the next one until you find one that you do understand.

5. Read the psalm you have chosen out loud two times.

6. Consider the following questions to help you reflect on the psalm. Write down—or draw a sketch about—some of your thoughts in your journal.

- What does this psalm tell me about God?
- How does this psalm fit (or not fit) my mood today?
- What is God saying to me in this psalm?
- What do I want to say back to God?

7. Choose a few words from the psalm that speak to your heart. It could be a phrase like "For great is your love, reaching to the heavens" (Psalm 57) or "How majestic is your name in all the earth!" (Psalm 8) or "Have mercy on me, O God" (Psalm 51).

Repeat the words out loud until you can say them without reading them. Then close your eyes and continue to say the words out loud (or say them silently, just moving your lips). Keep this up for a couple of minutes. Try to let the words "sink in" to your heart. Let them become the cry of your heart.

This may seem a little strange to you at first. But it can be a wonderful way to memorize bits of Scripture and meditate on God's Word. God can use these moments of meditation to draw you closer and to help you become more like Jesus in your everyday life.

Psalms That Express the Way We Feel ➤ ••••••••••••••••••➤

MY MOOD TODAY

	Happy, thankful	Sad, down, in need of encourage- ment	Angry	Afraid, in need of protection	Lonely or over- whelmed	Feeling far from God because of sin in my life
P S A L M S	8-9, 18-19, 23-24, 26, 29-30, 33-34, 40, 47-49, 62-63, 65-68, 71, 73, 75, 81, 84, 89-93, 95-101, 103-105, 107-108, 110-113, 115, 117, 122, 125, 127, 133-136, 138, 141, 144-150	4, 10, 13, 21-22, 27-28, 31, 39, 42-43, 56-57, 61, 64, 69-70, 74, 77, 88, 102, 116, 121, 130, 140	10, 13, 22, 37, 74, 142	7, 11-12, 16-17, 35, 46, 55-56, 59, 86, 118	3, 5, 10, 13, 20, 22, 27, 28, 31, 35, 41, 54-55, 59, 64, 69, 70, 74, 88, 109, 116, 121, 130, 140, 143	6, 14, 25, 32, 38-39, 43, 50-51, 84, 131, 139

Plan B:
The Jesus I Want to Know—Stories from the Gospels

What This Is About

Can you imagine living during the time of Jesus? Hearing him preach? Witnessing his miracles? Even talking to him or sharing a meal with him? If you have a good imagination and an open heart, you can experience all of these things through the stories of Matthew, Mark, Luke, and John. This three-week program will take you on an amazing journey with Jesus. It will help you to learn from and become more like Jesus.

Set a goal of daily Bible study for the next three weeks. If for some reason you miss a day or two, don't quit the program! Just pick up where you left off and keep going until the three weeks are up. Remember that the goal isn't to rack up Bible study time to impress God, your accountability partner, or anyone else! The goal is to get to know God better by listening to God speak to you.

What You Will Need

- a quiet, comfortable, private place

- a Bible (you may want to use an easy-to-understand version like the New Living Translation)

- a pen and journal

- about fifteen to twenty minutes of your day

- a willingness to listen to God

The Plan

1. Find a quiet, comfortable, private place where you can read, pray, and write in your journal.

2. Spend a minute or two quieting down. Close your eyes and take some slow, deep breaths. Sometimes listening to a soothing song can help you relax.

3. Pray. Ask God to meet you today. Ask God to help you say what's on your heart. Ask God to help you listen as God speaks to you through the Word and Spirit.

4. Choose a story to read from one of the gospels. The list of stories on the back of this page is a good place to start (or choose your own stories). Read them in any order, but stick to just one story per day.

5. Read the story out loud two times.

6. Use your imagination to put yourself into the story. Put yourself in the place of the person who met Jesus. Imagine yourself as a member of the crowd, watching one of Jesus' miracles. Imagine yourself as one of the people Jesus was teaching. You may want to read the story again, imagining yourself in it.

7. Consider the following questions to help you reflect on the story. Write down—or draw a sketch about—some of your thoughts in your journal.

- What would it have felt like to be the person in the story who met Jesus? Who was healed by Jesus? Who listened to Jesus?
- What might Jesus might be trying to show me or teach me through this story?
- How does this story make me feel? What does it make me think about?

8. Pray about whatever it is that Jesus might be teaching you or showing you through this story. Is he asking you to trust him more? Is he offering to heal a part of you that has been hurt? Is he assuring you that you can put your faith in him? If you're not sure what Jesus is telling you in the story, ask God to make it clear through the Holy Spirit. God will answer your prayer!

Stories About Jesus and Where to Find Them

Story	Bible Reference
The Baptism of Jesus	Matthew 3:13-17
Jesus' Temptation in the Desert	Luke 4:1-13
Jesus' First Miracle: Water to Wine	John 2:1-11
Nicodemus and Jesus	John 3:1-21
The Calling of the First Disciples	Luke 5:1-11
The Beatitudes	Matthew 5:3-12
The Healing of the Man by the Pool	John 5:1-9
The Centurion's Faith	Matthew 8:5-13
A Widow's Son Raised	Luke 7:11-17
Christ's Feet Anointed by a Woman	Luke 7:36-50
The Parable of the Sower	Mark 4:1-20
The Parables of the Treasure and Pearl	Matthew 13:44-46
Jesus Calms the Storm	Matthew 8:23-27
Healing of the Demon-Possessed Man	Mark 5:1-20
Healing of a Woman and a Girl	Luke 8:40-56
Feeding of the Five Thousand	John 6:4-13
Jesus Walks on Water	Matthew 14:24-33
Healing a Blind Man at Bethsaida	Mark 8:22-26
Jesus Forgives an Adulterous Woman	John 7:53-8:11
The Good Samaritan	Luke 10:25-37
Cost of Discipleship	Luke 14:25-35
Lazarus Raised from the Dead	John 11:1-44
Parables on Prayer	Luke 18:1-14
Little Children and the Kingdom	Mark 10:13-16
A Poor Widow's Gift	Luke 21:1-4

Plan C:
You're My Hero! Old Testament Bible Characters

What This Is About

Do you have a hero? Heroes can be important people in our lives. Our heroes often inspire us to be just like them. Heroes remind us that even though we're all human and we all make mistakes, we can still do some pretty important things with our lives. This three-week program focuses on some heroes of faith from the Bible. You will be asked to reflect on how you might want to be like them (think of their triumphs) and how you might choose NOT to be like them (think of their blunders).

Set a goal of daily Bible study for the next three weeks. If for some reason you miss a day or two, don't quit the program! Just pick up where you left off and keep going until the three weeks are up. Remember that the goal isn't to rack up Bible study time to impress God, your accountability partner, or anyone else! The goal is to get to know God better by listening to God speak to you.

What You Will Need

- a quiet, comfortable, private place

- a Bible (you may want to use an easy-to-understand version like the New Living Translation)

- a pen and journal

- about fifteen to twenty minutes of your day

- a willingness to listen to God

The Plan

1. Find a quiet, comfortable, private place where you can read, pray, and write in your journal.

2. Spend a minute or two quieting down. Close your eyes and take some slow, deep breaths. Sometimes listening to a soothing song can help you relax.

3. Pray. Ask God to meet you today. Ask God to help you say what's on your heart. Ask God to help you listen as God speaks to you through the Word and Spirit.

4. Choose a story about an Old Testament Bible character. You may use the list on the other side of this page or choose other stories you're interested in. If you choose characters from our list, you'll spend three days on each character. If a character really interests you and you want to read more about this person, that's fine too.

5. Read the story out loud two times.

6. Consider the following questions to help you reflect on the story. Write down—or draw a sketch about—some of your thoughts in your journal.

- In what ways did this character please God? Did he or she obey God, even when it was scary or hard? Did this person show faith in God in some way? How did the person show love and a desire to follow God?
- Did this character make any blunders in obeying God? If so, what were they? How did those blunders make the character act or feel? How did they make *me* feel about the character? Was I disappointed?
- What did I learn about God from this story?
- Did the story teach me anything about the ways in which I would like to grow or change?

7. Pray about the things you just wrote down in your journal. Talk to God about the story and how it made you feel. Ask God to give you whatever you feel you lack in your spiritual life—maybe things like more courage, more faith, or a servant's heart. God loves to give us these kinds of gifts.

Bible Characters and Where to Find Their Stories

Character	Day	Bible Reference
Abraham	1	Genesis 12:1-9; 13:1-18
	2	Genesis 18:1-15
	3	Genesis 22:1-19
Joseph	1	Genesis 37
	2	Genesis 39
	3	Genesis 45
Moses	1	Exodus 2
	2	Exodus 3-4:17
	3	Exodus 13:17-15:21
Joshua	1	Numbers 13:16-14:45
	2	Joshua 1
	3	Joshua 3-4
Deborah	1	Judges 4
Hannah	1	1 Samuel 1-2:11
David	1	1 Samuel 16
	2	2 Samuel 6
	3	2 Samuel 11-12
Elijah	1	1 Kings 17
	2	1 Kings 18:16-46
	3	2 Kings 2:1-18
Esther	1	Esther 1-2
	2	Esther 3-6
	3	Esther 7-10

My Commitment to Daily Bible Reading

I, _____, promise, to the best of my ability and with the help of the Holy Spirit and my accountability partner, to read the Bible once each day for the next three weeks. I understand that this has nothing to do with earning God's love for me, since God already loves me right now, just as I am. I do this daily Bible reading with thankfulness in my heart for what God has already done for me by sending Jesus to die for me on the cross.

I also commit to holding my accountability partner, _____, to his/her daily Bible reading by encouraging him/her, by praying regularly for him/her, and by otherwise helping in any way I can to help him/her keep his/her commitment. I also promise to be honest with my accountability partner when he/she asks me about how my daily Bible reading is going.

I understand that my signature below binds me to this contract and indicates my desire to grow closer to Jesus in my everyday life. I also understand that the Holy Spirit will bless me in this desire to grow spiritually.

I choose Plan _____ (A, B, C, or substitute your own).

_____   _____
signature of commitment maker   date

_____   _____
signature of accountability partner   date

Tips on How to be an ABSOLUTELY AWESOME Accountability Partner

Be honest!

Accountability without honesty doesn't work. If you haven't done your reading for a couple of days and your accountability partner asks you about it, tell the truth. This isn't always easy, but it is important!

Work out a plan for regular contact.

Maybe you'll see your partner regularly at school to ask how daily devotions are going. Maybe you'll need to call every other night to encourage your partner to keep his commitment. Decide ahead of time what works with your partner . . . what might be too much contact, and what might not be enough.

Think encouragement, not babysitting.

Don't get down on your partner for failing if she does. Brainstorm ways you could encourage your partner throughout the next three weeks.

Listen.

Making and keeping new commitments is hard work! So be quick to listen to your partner's frustrations and struggles. Sometimes all your partner will need is someone to listen without criticizing.

Pray.

Pray daily for your partner. Pray that God will bless and strengthen his or her commitment to grow in the spiritual discipline of daily Bible reading.

Listening to God ....

The Gentle Whisper of God ◄ ....

⁹*But the Lord said to him, "What are you doing here, Elijah?"*

¹⁰*Elijah replied, "I have zealously served the LORD God Almighty. But the people of Israel have broken their covenant with you, torn down your altars, and killed every one of your prophets. I alone am left, and now they are trying to kill me, too."*

¹¹*"Go out and stand before me on the mountain," the Lord told him. And as Elijah stood there, the Lord passed by, and a mighty windstorm hit the mountain. It was such a terrible blast that the rocks were torn loose, but the Lord was not in the wind. After the wind there was an earthquake, but the Lord was not in the earthquake. ¹²And after the earthquake there was a fire, but the Lord was not in the fire. And after the fire there was the sound of a gentle whisper. ¹³When Elijah heard it, he wrapped his face in a cloak and went out and stood at the entrance to the cave.*
—1 Kings 19:9-13 (New Living Translation)

👉 What's the surprise in this story?

👉 Why do you think God chose to speak to Elijah in a whisper instead of in the wind, earthquake, or fire?

👉 How does Elijah feel after hearing God speak in a gentle whisper?

👉 How do you think God "talks" to us today—in a big, booming voice or in a still, small voice? Explain.

👉 In the story, Elijah is "distracted" by the wind, earthquake, and fire. What are the top three distractions that prevent you from listening to God?

👉 What do we have to do if we want to hear God?

Listening to God: Drawing What I See

Have you ever noticed how some Bible passages give you really clear images or mental pictures? Take the psalms, for instance. They are often full of such pictures. This exercise uses a very familiar psalm to help you practice speaking and listening to God by drawing an image the psalm suggests to you. Nope, you don't have to be an artist or even like art to do this. It's easy! And it's a great way to really get into a Bible passage and hear God speak through it.

What to Do

1. Read Psalm 23 (printed below) through once.

   The Lord is my shepherd;
   I have everything I need.
   He lets me rest in green meadows;
   he leads me beside peaceful streams.
   He renews my strength.
   He guides me along right paths,
   bringing honor to his name.

   Even when I walk
   through the dark valley of death,
   I will not be afraid,
   for you are close beside me.
   Your rod and staff
   protect and comfort me.

   You prepare a feast for me
   in the presence of my enemies.
   You welcome me as a guest,
   anointing my head with oil.
   My cup overflows with blessings.
   Surely your goodness and unfailing love will pursue me
   all the days of my life,
   and I will live in the house of the Lord
   forever.

2. Say a short prayer. Ask God to help you listen for what God is saying to you in some part of the psalm today. Trust God to help you.

3. Read the psalm again. As you read, look for an image you can easily picture in your mind. The picture doesn't even have to be directly related to the psalm. If a word or phrase triggered a picture in your head that seems totally unrelated to the psalm, that's OK. Or maybe the picture is a fairly typical image out of an old children's storybook. It really doesn't matter—as long as it is a picture you can relate to. For example, maybe when you read the words "my cup overflows with blessings," you can see this huge cup with all sorts of good things spilling out of it. Out of the whole psalm, this may be the picture that sticks in your mind the most.

4. Sketch the picture that you have chosen. Don't worry about being a great artist or anything. Just do the best you can (use your own paper for this).

5. Now imagine yourself as a part of the picture. Sketch yourself into the scene, not just looking at it from the outside. For example, if the picture you chose was the cup running over, where are you in the picture? Are you the one holding the cup? Is God holding the cup? Are you the cup itself? Let your mind wander as you think about where you might find yourself in the picture.

6. Spend a minute or two thinking about this question: What might God be saying to me through this picture? On the back of your sketch, write a few sentences in answer to this question.

Listening to God: Writing What I Hear

Journaling is a great way to get your thoughts and feelings down on paper, as a help to yourself and as a prayer to God. In this listening experience, you will be asked to open your mind and heart to what God might be saying to you. Sometimes when you journal this way, especially at first, nothing pops into your mind and ends up on the page. But other times, this kind of "guided journaling" can result in surprising and faith-building results!

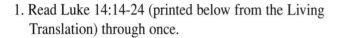

What to Do

1. Read Luke 14:14-24 (printed below from the Living Translation) through once.

   Hearing this, a man sitting at the table with Jesus exclaimed, "What a privilege it would be to have a share in the Kingdom of God!"

   Jesus replied with this illustration, "A man prepared a great feast and sent out many invitations. When all was ready, he sent his servant around to notify the guests that it was time for them to come. But they all began making excuses. One said that he had just bought a field and wanted to inspect it, so he asked to be excused. Another said he had just bought five pair of oxen and wanted to try them out. Another had just been married, so he said he couldn't come.

   "The servant returned and told his master what they had said. His master was angry and said, 'Go quickly into the streets and alleys of the city and invite the poor, the crippled, the lame, and the blind.' After the servant had done this, he reported, 'There is still room for more.' So the master said, 'Go out into the country lanes and behind the hedges and urge anyone you find to come, so that the house will be full. For none of those I invited first will get even the smallest taste of what I had prepared for them.'"

2. Say a short prayer. Ask God to open your heart and mind to what God wants to say to you through this parable today. Trust God to help you.

3. Read the parable again. As you read, ask yourself, How do I fit into this parable? Do I see myself in any of the characters in this story? Who? For example, maybe when you read about the people making

excuses instead of coming to the banquet, you thought, "That's me. I make excuses a lot when I want to get out of something."

4. Take one or two minutes (at the most) to write down your thoughts to the questions above. You don't need to write a lot—just jot down where you find yourself in the parable and why.

5. Now stop writing. Say a short prayer, asking God to show you what you can learn from this parable, especially the part of the parable that you found yourself in. This may seem a little strange, but ask anyway. Then wait quietly. Don't feel pressure to write something down right away, but as thoughts come to you, write them down. Write them as if God is speaking to you, not in your own voice. Here's an example of what that might look like: "My child (use your name), you need to stop making excuses about growing in your faith. I don't want you to begin growing next week, or next year, or in the summer when you won't see your friends as much. I want your heart now. I want you to come and join the great banquet that I have set out for you right now. No more excuses."

6. If you don't have anything to write after waiting and listening for a few minutes, don't worry! If your prayer was sincere, God will speak to you—maybe not now and maybe not in this way, but God will speak. God loves to communicate with us. Ask God to help you hear God's voice.

Praying for All It's Worth

Hailing the Chief

Note: This skit was adapted from "Hailing the Chief," *High Impact Worship Dramas,* © 1999 by John Duckworth, published by Group Publishing, Inc., P.O. Box 481, Loveland, CO 80539. Used by permission.

Roles

Narrator	President
Secretary	Homemaker
Stout man	Scared person
Young person	Elderly man
Woman	Child

Note: Feel free to assign more than one role to each person, if necessary.

The Scene

Set up the "stage" to resemble the way you imagine the Oval Office of the president of the United States might look, with a desk for the president (have him to one side so that the audience sees his profile and the side of the desk), a chair for those who will visit him, and a door for them to enter. You may represent the "door" with a strip of duct tape on the floor. You may also want to set up a secretary's desk or chair beyond the door with a "pretend" intercom on both desks. The narrator should stand off to the opposite side of the "stage." The president should be sitting in his chair, waiting. The secretary should be in the outer office, pretending to do secretarial work.

The Script

Narrator: He sat in the Oval Office, waiting. He waited, even though there was a stack of letters to sign, a cable to read, a press conference to prepare for, a briefing with the cabinet to attend, a tea for an ambassador in the Rose Garden. . . .

Looking up from his schedule, he smiled. Yes, there was a lot to do. But first, some people were coming—some very important people.

At least, *he* thought they were very important. That was why he kept inviting them to come to the Oval Office and talk with him. He longed to hear what was in their hearts and minds, to talk about how they felt, what they needed, and how they could help him accomplish his goals. . . .

Secretary: *[pretending to press on the intercom button in order to talk to the president in his office]* Mr. President . . . they're here, sir.

President: Ah, send the first one in, please. *[Leans forward in his chair, waiting. The door opens and a homemaker enters into the room. Without acknowledging the president's smile or outstretched hand, the home-maker plops down in the chair and shuts eyes tight.]*

Homemaker: *[speaks in a nasal, singsong voice]* Dear Mr. President, thank you for the world so sweet, thank you for the food we eat, thank you for the birds that sing, thank you, sir, for everything. Goodbye.

Narrator: Before the president could say a word in response, the visitor opened her eyes, got up, and walked right out the door. The president sighed. Why did it always seem to go like this?

President: *[pushing the intercom button]* Next, please.

[In comes a stout man wearing a tuxedo. He ignores the president's hand.]

Stout man: O thou chief executive who art in the White House *[the man clasps his hands together piously and looks at the ceiling]*, O thou in whom so much doth constitutionally dwell, upon whose desk hath been placed a most effective blotter *[motions toward the president's desk]*; incline thine ear toward thy most humble citizen, and grant that thy many entities may be manifoldly endowed upon the fruitful plain. . . .

[President winces, closes his eyes, and rubs his temples as if he has a headache.]

Stout man: *[continuing in a loud monotone]* And may thy thou dost harkeneth whatly didst shalt evermore in twain asunder . . .

President: Excuse me . . . but what . . . ?

Stout man: *[as the president begins to speak, the stout man begins to leave]* Goodbye. *[walks out]*

Narrator: The president sighed again.

President: *[speaking into the intercom again]* Next, please. *[Rises from his chair looking confused because he can't see the person who is entering the office now. The person crawls on hands and knees toward the empty chair but stays on the floor, on hands and knees.]*

Scared Person: *[blubbering, scared]* Oh, Mr. g-great and awful P-president! I am but a disgusting piece of filth in your presence. No, I am less than that! How dare I enter here? How dare I think that you would do anything but grind me into the floor!

President: *[motioning for the person to get up and offering his hand]* Please get up. You don't have to do that. I *want* to talk with you.

Narrator: But the visitor went on grovelling.

Scared person: *[whining]* I deserve only to be squashed under the weight of your mighty desk. I could never have received an invitation to talk with you. It must have been a mistake. How can you ever forgive me for breaking in like this? Oh, I'm so sorry, so sorry, so sorry. . . . *[Still on hands and knees, crawls out.]*

Narrator: The groaning faded down the hall. The president shook his head, then slowly pushed the intercom button.

President: Next.

[A young person enters wearing headphones and bobbing up and down to the music of a pocket stereo.]

Young person: Hey prez *[ignoring the president's outstretched hand]*, what's happening? *[pretends to look out the window]* Nice place you got here. I'm, like, so glad we could have this little chat, you know? You're not bad for an old dude, I guess. You don't bother me, I won't bother you, OK? Well, I've gotta go. Hang in there. *[walks out]*

Narrator: The president drummed his fingers on his desk. . . .

President: *[wearily]* Next.

[An elderly man marches in, staring at a piece of paper in his hand. He too ignores the president's outstretched hand.]

Elderly man: *[impatiently]* Mr. President, *[he keeps his eyes on the piece of paper]* I want there to be a parking space waiting for me when I go downtown this afternoon. Not a parallel parking space either—one that I can drive right into. Not one with a parking meter. You can see to it that none of those meter maids gives me a ticket. Now, this is important!

President: *[clearing his throat and still speaking politely]* Speaking of important, how do you feel about my program to feed the hungry? Would you like to have a part in . . . ?

Elderly man: *[interrupting]* And another thing! I lost my best golf club! A putter. Can't remember where I put it. Now, you find it for me, will you? Got to have that club before Saturday. I know you can do it. Goodbye. *[leaves]*

Narrator: The president slumped in his chair.

President: *[sounding discouraged]* Next.

[A young woman enters slowly. She looks like a sleepwalker—eyes nearly shut, jaw slack, her feet dragging. She yawns and slides into the chair.]

Woman: *[head drooping, yawning throughout]* Dear . . . Mr. . . . President . . . I know I should talk to you when I'm more . . . awake . . . but I've got so many things to do . . . so . . . sleepy. . . . There was something I was going to say. . . . What is . . . ? I was going to say . . . uh . . . *[her head drops to her chest and she starts to snore]*

[The president buzzes the secretary, who steps in.]

President: Could you help this young lady out? *[sighs]*

Secretary: Certainly, Mr. President.

President: *[to the secretary, who is helping the young woman out]* How many do we have left?

Secretary: I'm sorry, sir, but as usual, most of the people you sent invitations to said they were too busy to talk. They had to watch TV, wax the car, do the dishes . . .

President: *[dejected]* Oh! Isn't there *anyone* out there?

Secretary: There is one, sir . . . but you wouldn't want to talk with this person.

President: Why not?

Secretary: Because it's just a child, Mr. President.

President: *[shrugging]* May as well show the child in.

[A child enters shyly. Looks around the room, eyes wide.]

Child: Are—are you really the *president?*

President: *[smiling]* I really am! *[offers his hand to the child]*

Child: *[reaches up and shakes president's hand, then sits down and folds hands in lap and waits]*

President: *[watches as the child does this, amazed]* Isn't there . . . something you want to tell me? Something you'd like to recite, or ask for, or say?

Child: *[thinks for a moment]* Yes, I guess there is.

President: Well, what is it?

Child: *[smiling at the president]* Thank you for inviting me. *[pauses]* That's all.

Narrator: When the president heard that, he couldn't seem to say anything at all for a while. All he could do was smile. But then they talked and talked for the longest, most wonderful time.

How David Talked to God

Instructions:

Decide who will be Reader 1 and who will be Reader 2. Take turns reading your parts, stopping after each person reads to write (on the chart) what you think David might have been feeling when he wrote that part of his prayer.

All Scripture in this chart is from the Holy Bible: New Living Translation.

Psalm 22 (Reader 1)	Psalm 23 (Reader 2)	David's Feelings
Verses 1-2, 7-8 My God, my God! Why have you forsaken me? Why do you remain so distant? Why do you ignore my cries for help? Every day I call to you, my God, but you do not answer. Every night you hear my voice, but I find no relief. Everyone who sees me mocks me. They sneer and shake their heads, saying, "Is this the one who relies on the LORD? Then let the LORD save him! If the LORD loves him so much, let the Lord rescue him."		
	Verses 1-3a The LORD is my shepherd; I have everything I need. He lets me rest in green meadows; he leads me beside peaceful streams. He renews my strength.	

Psalm 22 (Reader 1)	Psalm 23 (Reader 2)	David's Feelings
Verses 11-15 Do not stay so far from me, 　for trouble is near, 　and no one else can help me. My enemies surround me like a 　herd of bulls; 　fierce bulls of Bashan have 　hemmed me in! Like roaring lions attacking their 　prey, 　they come at me with open 　mouths. My life is poured out like water, 　and all my bones are out of 　joint. My heart is like wax, 　melting within me. My strength is dried up like 　sunbaked clay. 　My tongue sticks to the roof of 　my mouth. 　You have laid me in the dust and 　left me for dead.		
	Verses 3b-4a The LORD guides me along right 　paths, 　bringing honor to his name. Even when I walk 　through the dark valley of death, I will not be afraid, 　for you are close beside me.	
Verses 19-21 O LORD, do not stay away! 　You are my strength; come 　quickly to my aid! Rescue me from a violent death; 　spare my precious life from 　these dogs. Snatch me from the lions' jaws, 　and from the horns of these wild 　oxen.		

Psalm 22 (Reader 1)	Psalm 23 (Reader 2)	David's Feelings
	Verse 4b Your rod and your staff protect and comfort me.	

Verses 26b-28
All who seek the LORD will praise
   him.
Their hearts will rejoice with
   everlasting joy.
The whole earth will acknowledge
   the LORD and return to him.
People from every nation will bow
   down before him.
For the LORD is king!
   He rules all the nations.		

	Verse 5
	You prepare a feast for me
	   in the presence of my enemies.
	You welcome me as a guest,
	   anointing my head with oil.
	   My cup overflows with blessings.	

Verses 29-31
Let the rich of the earth feast and
   worship.
   Let all mortals—those born to
   die—bow down in his presence.
Future generations will also serve
   him.
   Our children will hear about the
   wonders of the Lord.
His righteous acts will be told to
   those yet unborn.
   They will hear about everything
   he has done.		

	Verse 6
	Surely your goodness and unfailing
	   love will pursue me
	   all the days of my life,
	and I will live in the house of the
	   LORD
	   forever.	

Keep Track!

You are invited to keep a record of your prayers for one week.
The chart below will help you do that.

- Keep on praying. No matter what happens, always be thankful, for this is God's will for you who belong to Christ Jesus. (1 Thessalonians 5:17-18)

- The eyes of the Lord watch over those who do right; his ears are open to their cries for help. (Psalm 34:15)

- God will surely listen to our prayer because of Christ our Lord. This is what he has promised us in his Word. (Heidelberg Catechism Q&A 117)

Day	Time You Prayed	Reason You Prayed (Praise, thanks, confession?)	For Whom? (Self, others)

Use the space below to write down some of your reactions to the following questions.

- After a week of keeping track of your prayer life, what patterns do you notice? Do you find that you pray more at certain times of the day? More for others than for yourself? Mostly praise and never any confession? Maybe you would like to add more praise to your prayers, or spend more time praying for other people.

- What have you learned about daily prayer in the past week? About yourself?

Session 6
Encouraging Each Other

A Young Man Who Needed Encouragement

Who was Timothy? Well, besides someone who had two Bible books named after him, he was an ordinary person who grew up in the city of Lystra, in what we now call Turkey. His mom was a Jewish Christian who carefully taught her son the stories and teachings of the Old Testament. Timothy may have committed his life to Christ when the apostle Paul visited Lystra on his first missionary journey. Paul liked young Timothy and later called him "my true son in the faith" (1 Timothy 1:2).

When Paul visited Lystra a second time, he invited Timothy to go with him on his journey to faraway cities that Timothy had never seen before. This may sound like fun, but remember that Paul was often beaten with whips, run out of town by angry mobs, pelted with stones, and thrown into prison—all for telling people about Jesus. Timothy shared in those dangers. He traveled with Paul to Ephesus, Macedonia, Corinth, Asia Minor, and even all the way to Jerusalem.

Eventually, Paul decided to leave Timothy in Ephesus, the biggest city in Asia, famous for its beautiful temple of the goddess Diana. "Timothy, you're going to be in charge of the Christian church in Ephesus," Paul said. "Take good care of it while I'm away."

That wouldn't be easy. The church in Ephesus was growing fast and needed a strong leader. Some of the older people in the church probably wouldn't trust someone as young as Timothy. And there were problems in the church: some church members were

teaching false things about Jesus. So you can see that Paul really trusted Timothy. He knew that Timothy would make a good leader even though Timothy was still a young man without a lot of experience.

Paul wrote Timothy letters to give him instructions and to encourage him. Why do you think Timothy needed encouragement? How do you think he felt as the new leader of the church at Ephesus?

Paul Encourages Timothy

Dear Timothy,

I am sending you this letter. You are my true son in the faith. May God the Father and Christ Jesus our Lord give you grace, mercy, and peace.

Stay there in Ephesus. That is what I told you to do when I went into Macedonia. I want you to command certain people not to teach things that aren't true. . . .

My son Timothy, I give you these teachings. They are in keeping with the prophecies that were once made about you. By following them, you can fight the good fight. Then you will hold on to faith. You will hold on to a good sense of what is right and wrong. . . .

You were brought up in the truths of the faith. You received good teaching. You followed it. . . .

Here is a saying you can trust. You can accept it completely. We work hard for it. Here is the saying. We have put our hope in the living God. He is the Savior of all people. Most of all he is the Savior of those who believe.

Command those things. Teach them. Don't let anyone look down on you because you are young. Set an example for the believers in what you say and in how you live. Also set an example in how you love and in what you believe. Show the believers how to be pure.

Until I come, spend your time reading Scripture out loud to one another. Spend your time preaching and teaching. Don't fail to use the gift the Holy Spirit gave you. He gave it to you through a message from God. It was given when the elders placed their hands on you.

Keep on doing these things. Give them your complete attention. Then everyone will see how you are coming along. Be careful of how you live and what you believe. Never give up. Then you will save yourself and those who hear you.

—Paul (1 Timothy 1:2-3, 18-19; 4:6, 9-16, New International Reader's Version)

Imagine . . .

that you are Timothy. Underline the parts of Paul's letter that you find most helpful or encouraging.

Encouragement Tips

OK, so now we've looked at how Paul encouraged his good friend Timothy. What can we learn about encouragement from Paul's example and from our own experiences? With others in your group, make a list of "encouragement tips"—things to keep in mind as we encourage others by our actions and words.

WANTED
Encouragers!

Chances are, you know someone who could really use some cheering up—a word of appreciation, some praise, a thoughtful and unselfish act of kindness. Think of someone you could encourage this week. Write the person's name below, along with a brief note about what you could say or do. Then make a commitment to say it or do it this week!

The person I plan to encourage is

_____

Here's what I plan to do:

_____

_____

_____

On the Journey (Again)

Do you remember the story of the prodigal son from the first session of this course? In that session, did you place yourself	• at home with the younger brother, restless and wanting your freedom? • in the faraway country, having a great time? • in the pigpen, wishing you were at home? • on the road back home? • with the elder brother at home?

A few weeks have gone by since then. Maybe you started a Bible reading program or kept a prayer chart. Maybe you've learned to listen to God in some new ways. Maybe you're especially grateful for someone who has encouraged you in your faith.

Think back to the story of the prodigal son as the story of your relationship with God. Have you changed your position in the story? For instance, do you feel you're a little farther on the road home to your heavenly Father? In other words, has anything happened that has helped you grow spiritually? Use the space below to jot down your comments.

Now think about a roadblock that keeps you from traveling towards the Father or at least slows your progress down the road home. It might be something like not talking to God very often or seldom reading God's Word. Or maybe it's a struggle with bad language or a bad temper or hatred toward someone. Maybe it's fear of not being accepted by your friends at school. Or maybe you think being a Christian means not having any fun.

Whatever it is, please write it on the lines below.

_____

_____

Your group leader and others in the class are doing the same thing you are. They all have weak areas too.

Remember that God promises to bless us with strength and courage when we ask for it. So as you pray this week, ask God for strength, endurance, and courage as you continue your journey home to the Father.